EMIN GRBO

How An Egg-Timer App Got Me Every Job

a junior developer's battle-plan

Before we dig into this, I cannot go any further without thanking my wife and daughter for either knowingly or unknowingly supporting me in all my efforts and goals. I am a hard person to live with, and they make it more enjoyable than one could ever ask for.

I grew up surrounded by extremely supportive parents and a crazy creative sister which helped me shape my current views of the world. Without all of them I am not sure if I would be here where I am.

Thank you!

Contents

Foreword

I'm not too fond of book intros and forewords, however, I do know people are used to that and almost expect it. Additionally, as this book heavily relies on establishing my professional background, it is almost necessary.

I am Emin Grbo, born in Zadar, Croatia. My father and sister are born in Bosnia, and my mother is from Serbia. I live in Norway. Is that important? No.

See...I told you.

What this book is

This book will share my journey of entering the iOS world and highlight the tools and strategies I utilized to successfully land every job I applied for.

Admittedly, it may come across as a boast, but I struggle to find an alternative way to present my approach without saying, "Look, it works, and here's the evidence." Regardless of whether it seems like boasting or not, the facts remain true. My genuine hope is that you will find value in this book.

> *This book is not exclusively meant for iOS developers, although some action items **are** specific to app makers. Feel free to adapt it to your preferred technology stack.*

The main reason I'm doing this is to help other junior developers break into the tech industry with as little pain as possible. Getting your first job is always the toughest, but everything that follows becomes at least 80% easier.

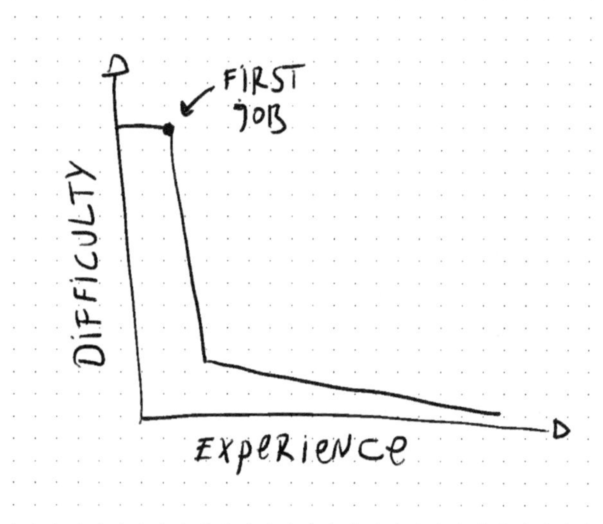

I'm not an avid reader or writer, so I'll do my best to communicate my thoughts clearly. As a programmer, I understand that excessive "context" isn't crucial. What matters most are clear steps and instructions on how to accomplish this goal, which I will provide. To reinforce this claim, I'll even offer a **checklist** for your next job hunt. Tough to get more direct than that.

Once I cover my past and describe how I navigated the **tutorial land** to eventually land a job, I will dig into the best approach for **searching** and **applying** for your first job. The **Egg Timer** app, which I will discuss later in the book, plays a significant role in this process. However, before we get to that, we need to cover some fundamental basics and address certain "state of mind" considerations.

While following the checklist will take you 70% of the way there, it's often necessary to get as many % as you can get your hands on.

> *This book doesn't primarily focus on concrete code implementations. Instead, it places emphasis on cultivating the right mindset when applying for jobs. It provides actionable advice to assist you in your job hunt. By taking this approach, I believe the book will remain timeless, rather than being tied to a specific technology or period.*

Note

One thing you should know about me is that I tend to dislike the "academic" way of writing. It's not that there's anything inherently wrong with it, but personally, I prefer to be plain and direct. This style may not always flow smoothly, but I find it easier to digest. It feels like I'm talking to you right now, rather than meticulously constructing each sentence for ten minutes.

As a result, it might get a bit chaotic at times. However, a good way to describe it is something I read in Pieter Levels' book "Make," where he refers to it as his "brain dump." Essentially, it's a direct expression of my thoughts on the subject. While the wording may not be perfect, **the ideas are sound.**

Let's go

<u>You are here, and that is what matters. With that, let's dig into it!</u>

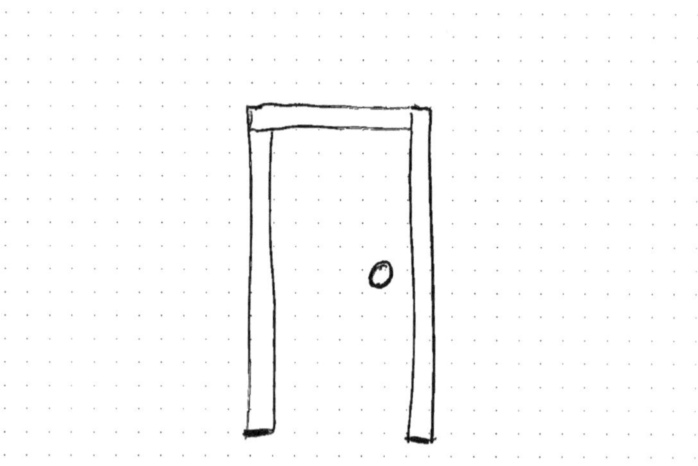

Are you exaggerating?

Let me put your mind at ease. No, I am not exaggerating.

This app, at the time of writing, got me 7 interviews applied for and 7 job offers. This does not mean I switched 7 jobs in the past 4 years as an iOS developer, that would be mental. It simply means that I reached the "offer" stage in the interviewing process, but for various reasons, I declined them.

If you're curious, *I did switch 2 jobs.*

I

Hello World

My pre–iOS experience.
Not too related to the book title itself, but as any good
story, it needs some foundations so you would
understand where I am coming from.

1

Who are you?

How it all started

My professional career starts in 2007, when I applied for a "Flash Developer" job opening. If you think I knew Flash at all, or what it is, you would have something in common with my future employer. Why did I apply then? If I am being 100% honest, I did it because:

1. It sounded cool.
2. I needed the money.

I applied for an interview and spent the next 7 days *living* and *breathing* Flash. Mostly watching YouTube tutorials made by 12-year-old kids. If you think I am joking, believe me, I wish I was **too**.

> *If you are not familiar with Flash, it's a technology that dominated the web from the early 2000's until maybe 2015. It was used to produce animated banners, websites, and even games! It was cool at that time.*

I got the job by the skin of my teeth and started learning about how banners work and what people like to see online, but maybe more importantly, what they hate. I just recently realized how this affected my further career and **shaped my understanding of first impressions.**

First level "up"

After gaining a few months of experience in Flash, the company made some unfortunate business decisions that led to its downfall. As a result, I found myself once again searching for a job.

I applied for 2 jobs. Worker in a bookstore, and a forklift driver. **I deliberately applied for these "easy" jobs because I needed some money while searching for a more substantial job.** I regret to inform you that the only job I *ever* failed at, was getting that forklift driver job. It haunts me to this day and honestly I do really feel sorry for not getting it. Work hours were 2am–6am, in an empty warehouse. I know right!?

Putting jokes aside, I genuinely appreciate **why** the hiring person turned me down. Their reasoning was along the lines of, "You're in college, and I understand that you need the money, but this job could potentially divert your focus from your academic studies, and I don't want that burden." While I'm not saying they were necessarily correct, I truly **commend** their effort to look out for my well-being.

However, I did manage to land a rather dull job at a bookstore. The pay was **extremely low**, and the only perk was a discount at a local shop. While working there, I decided to apply for two other jobs, aiming higher this time: Yellow Pages and "The Agency". Although I had no idea **who** "The Agency" was, their ad was written in English, leading me to believe they must be good, or just "better".

A week later, I received calls for interviews from both companies simultaneously. Yikes! I had to make a decision, and I usually don't take the "**shotgun approach**." So, I decided to attend only one interview and cancel the other.

When I opened the websites of both companies, Yellow Pages had an **overwhelming** amount of words and colors on their site (keep in mind it was 2008). On the other hand, "The Agenc had a simple website with just three sections: work, news, and careers.

I ultimately chose the latter.

Agency work

While interviewed for tho role at "The Agency", I took a very big risk. I told them my current salary is 720€. It was actually 180€, but I really thought it would pay of if they wanted me, which it did. Got offered a sweet 800€ and took the job on the spot. CH-CHING!

In case you are interested, I said 720 as 700 it way too round of a number, and 720 sounds like something you would not make up. Not saying it was some jedi-mind trick thing, but I like to think it helps remove some doubt if present.

During my time at "The Agency", I had the opportunity to dig into the workings of the human mind and witness firsthand how we can influence it through harmless advertisements and visuals. I was involved in creating a **wide range of materials**, including print materials, TV animations, billboards, fliers, and more.

I even managed to write an ad script for MasterCard which took several awards and was well-received overall. Exciting times!

https://www.youtube.com/watch?v=hsI_nu7UaYw

(kinda weird posting a link inside a book that might be printed but what can I do.)

Market Crash and freelance

Do you remember what happened in 2009? The **financial crisis**, banks collapsing, and all that **chaos**. It took some time for the impact to reach Serbia, but when it finally did, it hit hard. Or at least, companies used this as a good excuse to **"clear the ranks"**.

I was the youngest person in the company, easily ten years younger than anyone else. Given the circumstances, I felt that if anyone were to be fired, it would likely be me. To stay ahead of the situation, I took matters into my own hands and **approached the boss** directly, volunteering to be let go.

My initial reasoning was to maintain a positive relationship with them and avoid any hard feelings. Additionally, I had been eager to explore freelance opportunities, so this seemed like a half-open door for that kind of switch.

This paid off even more than I thought it would. Soon after, I was hired as an external associate, earning the same salary but working only 20% of the hours. A **BIG** win on my end as you can imagine.

Freelance was **very lucrative** and I was very dumb, not saving a single buck for quite time but basically drinking and eating it all. It wasn't until my wife joined me in freelancing that we began to see double the earnings and started saving some money.

Our freelance work involved collaborating with agencies, working with our own clients, and taking on projects through platforms like UpWork (formerly Elance). During this time, I had the pleasure of working with WhaleShark, **the most awarded** UpWork agency in the Balkans.

Let' get to iOS

This approach worked well for me until 2018, when I grew tired of creating visually appealing app designs only to hand off the rest of the development work to someone else. So, naturally, I decided to dive into learning coding languages.

To decide which platform to work on, I googled "**coding syntax**" and glanced over random code snippets. I literally just looked at images of code.

This, and other things that I do really seem overly simplistic and down right silly, but when you think about it, wouldn't you want to LIKE what you see if you are looking at it each day? To me it seemed like an extremely important thing.

I strongly believe in the importance of **simplifying** ideas and experiences that we encounter in our daily lives. Despite our mind's tendency to complicate things, our existence is fundamentally grounded in basic reasoning.

From my heavily scientific research(the googling), two languages popped up, **Ruby** and **Swift**. You would presume that Swift won, *but not initially.* I started learning Ruby, and loved it. Then I saw Ruby on Rails, barfed, and **then** started learning Swift.

At this point I am 33 years old and know *zero* about programming. A literal 0.

iOS Career

A year later, I applied for a job using my very first app, a simple egg timer that you'll hear more about in this book. I got the job and began working as a lone iOS developer responsible for maintaining three active apps on the store.

Simultaneously, I worked on implementing **new features** and developing fresh apps. It was **challenging**, but I was fortunate to have an incredibly friendly and supportive environment where I thrived.

A year later, I applied for a job at **TIDAL** and relocated to Norway. And yes, you guessed it right, the egg-timer app came to my rescue once again. I have been working there ever since. During my time at TIDAL, I had several interviews where I relied on my trusty egg-timer app to help me navigate the hiring process.

I am writing this book for one **simple reason**. During *every interview* I've had, I either managed to skip the take-home assignment or learned from hiring managers that the app played a **significant** role in the hiring process. One hiring manager even told me, "you should write a blog about this app."

So, I took their advice and decided to write a whole book.(blogs seem fleeting) But it's not **just about the app**—it covers the entire adventure and mindset required to **navigate** your way towards a job in tech.

I believe I have valuable insight to share in that area, and that it would surely aid you in your quest.

II

The Adventure Begins

The process of getting started, where to learn, how to learn and how to move towards that inevitable first app which will aid you in your job hunt. Let's go!

2

Tutorial Land

Once I had my eyes set on the language, I did some digging and found several really good **sources for learning**. There wasn't such ample amount of books out there like today, but still, you had some options.

And now, let me share my **first mistake**. I came across a very serious book, over 1000 pages long, highly academic, and considered **THE** go-to resource. Determined, I embarked on reading it at a leisurely pace, hoping to grasp every concept.

Spoiler, I did not.

Even after **several months** of reading, writing, and repeating, I still couldn't confidently explain how to write a proper Table-View or understand what **delegates** were all about. The reason? It simply wasn't the right fit for me. Now, please don't ask me the title of that book—because it's **not about labeling it as bad**. It just didn't **resonate** with me.

And that's the beauty of it! You have the power to choose the tutorial or book that **works best for you**. If you prefer **videos**, great! If not, dive into **reading**. And if that doesn't work, find a **coding buddy** and learn together. Experiment, try, repeat.

Do whatever it takes to get from point A to point B. The path is **yours to discover!**

> *Learning is an incredibly **individual process**, and what works for one person may not work for another. Don't hesitate to **voice out** that a particular learning style doesn't work for you. Remember, your ultimate goal is **to learn**. Therefore, it's important to be able to distinguish between a tutorial that **clicks with you** and one that **doesn't**.*

After reading that book, I was **devastated**. I found myself questioning, **"Am I dumb?"** I had always believed I was at least somewhat intelligent, but this book left me feeling lost and unsure of how to approach writing a simple app.

Revelation

Fortunately, my next search led me to **Angela Yu's** course on Udemy.

> *While I won't mention the specific resource that didn't work for me, I will gladly share the ones that did. The reason for this is that I always encourage sharing good experiences and resources, while avoiding to "throw shade" on the ones that I did not align with.*

During her introduction, Angela made a profound statement: **"I will not teach you HOW to do it, but WHY."** In that moment, my mind clicked like never before. I realized that I had been blindly following code without truly understanding the reasons behind its functionality! I knew how to write the code, but I had never stopped to ask myself **why** it worked the way it did.

From that point on, progress took on a whole new pace. Each day, I absorbed new concepts and **placed them in their proper context**. If there was something I didn't fully grasp, I would take a step back and repeat the work until I understood it. I vividly recall revisiting topics like closures multiple times, as they were still tricky to get. Looking back I realize that there was no need to repeat more than once though. If it is not clear in the moment, set a **TODO** and come back to it later.

> *When learning, don't worry about trying to understand every single detail. It's rare for complete comprehension to happen right away.*
>
> *To understand **MOST OF IT** should be your goal. **Complete understanding** comes only after several practical applications in code and rinse-repeat approach. Because if you understand most of it, you know how to search for it on Stack Overflow, and that is what being a developer is all about.*

As I started to grasp some of the ideas from the book I was reading previously, it dawned on me that it was intended for readers with at least a **basic** understanding of coding. It wasn't meant for someone like me, who had zero introduction and no tech background whatsoever. So the main reason it did not work for me is that I was not fully ready for it.

Time to go

Tutorial land is a fun and easy place to learn. Someone tells you what to write and how to write it, and you just **follow along**. Don't worry your pretty little head about the next steps, like making a network call or naming a class. You just rinse, repeat, and show up tomorrow.

But at some point, you must leave this land, **no matter the cost**. It may seem easy for experienced developers, but I vividly remember standing at the exit, tempted to stay for just five more tutorials, just two more concepts. It never gets easier, **but you have to do it**. Sit up straight, take a sip of your coffee, and **close that browser.**

3

The Grind

Now turn your browser back on, as you need to start making your app.

Crash and Burn

Once you leave Tutorial Land, a sense of **dread** may wash over you.

"Where do I even start?"

"How do I create a project again?"

"Do I save it on my desktop or create a separate folder?"

These questions are valid and important. Now, it's up to you to **make the decisions**. Go ahead, make mistakes, learn from them, and try again. It's time for you to crash and burn.

You have the right to make mistakes. Just out of Tutorial Land, now is the perfect time to stumble. The more errors you make now, the better developer you'll become, and the fewer mistakes you'll make at your first job.

However, please keep in mind that this app, whatever it may be, will be bad. Like, really awfully, riddled with bugs, "i do not want to even look at it" bad. And that's okay. Do your best to make it as good as you can, knowing that you can always fix or refactor it later, or even **choose to forget about it altogether**.

Alternatively, you could save it for the day when you become a CTO and use it as an example to inspire your new junior developers. A bad example mind you.

"Just think, if I can create this app and become a CTO, then you can too!"

> *During this stage, it is crucial to forgive yourself. Don't aim to create a mindless app, but also don't fret if it's not perfect. The paramount goal is to create as many things as possible, repeatedly.*

Rinse and Repeat

Once you've completed your first app, the real fun begins. **Repeat the process**, but this time, create another app, and then another. This repetition is a tried and true method for **building habits**.

While most of these habits will be good, some **bad ones** will surely develop. Don't worry, they **can** be fixed. In fact, they need to exist in order for you to replace them with new, positive habits.

When doing this, don't simply repeat the same type of app using the same technologies. Explore different areas. Instead of making another todo-app, focus on maps, notifications, images, or anything that interests you. To save time, keep them as simple as possible. They don't need to be fully developed apps ready for the world. Consider each app as a small feature within a larger app.

This approach will allow you to **start over** multiple times in a short period. When we start over, we start thinking of "what can i do better than the last time". Utilize that basic human nature to enhance your developer skills.

Think of your knowledge as a tree, with branches representing different skills. It doesn't make sense to have just one strong branch. Create a reasonable number of branches (types of apps) and develop them to a level where they are usable and good enough to branch out into new areas.

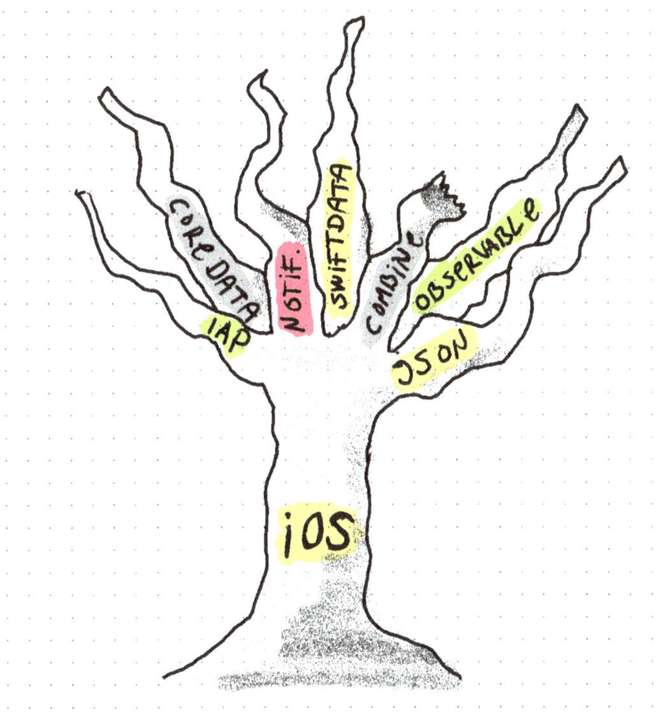

iOS tree of knowledge

To draw a comparison with the previous step, when you were making an app just for the sake of it, the complexity and functionality didn't matter much. But this time, your app **should be** almost good enough to be on the store, but has only one functionality.

A really easy way to grasp this is to imagine an app with 5 tabs, but instead of being a one app, you will make 5 apps, one for each tab. This removed the complexity of connecting all screens together which will come later.

After creating several apps, you'll start feeling that you're getting closer to your goal. Your confidence grows, and you'll be ready to move on to the **next step!**

> Focus on forgiving yourself for things you aren't yet aware of or find too complex right now. Fix obvious mistakes and ensure there are no glaring bugs.

4

First App

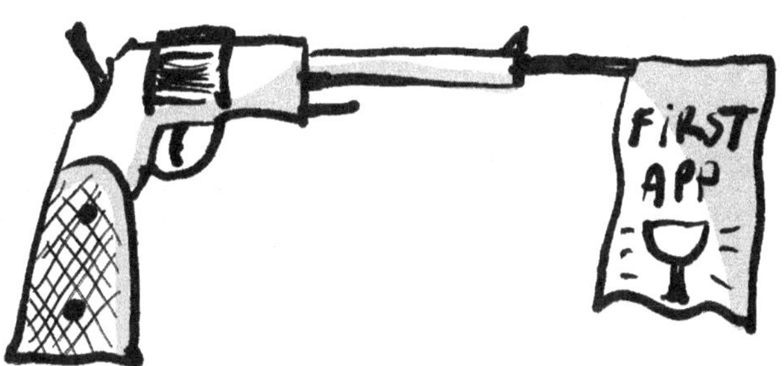

Prep

This is it. After the grind, you've reached the most crucial part of your **future hiring process**. Whether you're a junior developer or a seasoned professional searching for your next role, I firmly believe that this step holds **80%** of the reasons why you'll get noticed, remembered, and invited to at least the first round. After all, this whole book is about **THE** app!

The reason behind this belief becomes clear if you try to switch places with the hiring manager. You have twenty CVs in front of you - who do you invite? Names are all the same, age is usually not an issue, and **experience** emerges as the primary parameter. You may have **little to no experience**, leaving you at the bottom, but what about the **heart**?

At the end of the day, we're all human. The person reviewing these CVs is also human (hopefully), with their own emotions and character. And that, my friend, is our **golden ticket**! Your CV needs to confidently raise its hand and say, **"Put me in, coach!"**

> *Do not forget that people looking at these bunch of PDF are people with emotions and humor. Do something to stand out and make them remember you even as an interesting applicant, whatever you do to catch their gaze, is a win. Kinda like "no bad press" approach, but please do not do anything **scandalous**.*

The idea

To create an app, you first need an idea. It's crucial to choose a simple idea that can be packed with features. The "**secret**" lies in the fact that if an app is initially simple, like an egg-timer, adding various features can even appear humorous and **over-engineered**.

When people see an egg-timer, they expect simplicity or mediocrity. But when they encounter bold design and clever features, they might think, **"You know what, this is cool!"**

So, start by brainstorming something you're passionate about or something that captures your interest. Whether it's a timer, a movie title generator app, or a weather app, the key is to infuse it with **quirkiness**.

Add a clever twist, bold design, and captivating icon—our goal is to spark curiosity and entice users to **explore** the app.

A great example of this is the **CARROT** weather app. While there are thousands of weather apps available, CARROT stands out because of its **passion and humor**. This unique approach propelled it to the top of the AppStore.

Brian Mueller went above and beyond with the app's capabilities, making it a remarkable achievement. The general idea is clear: creating something exceptional is no easy task, but CARROT weather app proves it can be done.

Make it simple, make it quirky!

CARROT App Screenshots

*Take some time to **reflect on this**. The app idea should resonate with you and be something you genuinely care about. It doesn't have to be groundbreaking; just make it **personal**, something you absolutely love to talk about!*

5

Runny-Egg

Runny-Egg

To get the gears turning, let's take a look at the app that this entire book revolves around.

Runny-Egg! – https://apps.apple.com/no/app/runnyegg/id149 2171626

21:11
Search
10:00
hard
start

There aren't many elements on the screen, but that's expected for an egg timer. It's simple and straightforward: you select the type of egg you want and start the timer. There are no unnecessary obstacles or complicated steps to fulfill the app's main purpose. **Remember this** when working on your own app.

> *Ensure that the primary use-case remains clean and user-friendly.*

Demonstrating this app without a video can be challenging, but as you swipe left and right, the visual representation of the egg changes. I achieved this by utilizing Lottie, an **animation library from AirBnB** combined with a simple scrollView.

I absolutely adore the way it feels, and even after all these years, I have no desire to make any big alterations. If you want to experience it firsthand, you can find it on the store.

The Secret Sauce

What sets this app apart is its **multitude of features.**

While it may appear to be just an egg-timer on the surface, it actually offers so much more in terms of functionality.

- In-App-Purchases
- Lottie animations
- Audio player (for custom notifications in-app)
- Background Timers (this is a cool story on how timers work)
- Custom Haptics
- Local Notifications

- Custom fonts
- Alternative Icons
- Remote DB (a simple table with editable text fields)
- JSON fetch
- JSON parsing
- and more...

That's why it's essential for you to present it as **more than meets the eye**. This app showcases various concepts which you, as a developer, **can accomplish**. The fact that it looks cool is just the cherry on top.

> When developing your app, start with **simplicity** but include a few features that showcase your **capabilities**. The more concepts you incorporate, the better. Use visuals to appeal to non-tech recruiters and technical elements to impress the tech-savvy folks. Win them both, and you got yourself a J.O.B.!

Here are a few additional screens of the app. While I could go into the design details, this app, as much as it means to me, isn't **THAT** extraordinary. What truly sets it apart is the idea and the "secret sauce" mentioned earlier. **Make it flashy, but also cool.**

I won't pretend that I used any mind tricks or made super smart moves when it comes to my design approach. I simply tried to arrange pixels on the screen in a way that I find pleasing to the eye. The rise of **skeuomorphic** design, which was a cool style at the time, influenced my main approach.

The Icon

To make your app complete you cannot forget about the **icon**.
Do whatever you feel is best, but make sure that it works, and
that it is not **too generic**. If you decide to have a simple icon and
a base color around it, so be it. But consider investing time and
money into an icon that really **POPS**.

It brings me great joy to tell you that the Runny-Egg app icon
earned a spot in Michael Flarup's "The iOS App Icon Book", a
collection of neat iOS icons over the years.

6

Recap

Let's revise all the things you need for this app to work.

- A simple app with a basic idea that can be built upon
- At least four additional features that are not necessary for
  the app to function but add extra value

- Bold UX decisions that enhance user experience
- A snappy app icon that catches attention
- A memorable name that sticks with users

When selecting features, prioritize **usefulness** that demonstrates your workplace usability. Refer to the chapter "Junior Dev Checklist" for more details.

Do this methodically and plan as much as you can before you start to code. Since you're not yet fast at coding, the more problems you solve in planning, the better.

Don't add features just for the sake of it. Make sure they make sense. For instance, local notifications work well for a timer, but remote notifications may be unnecessary.

> *Write down your plan on paper and make sure to cover all the angles before doing actual coding. This planning process is crucial for handling tasks in the future and determining the scope of work.* **Having a task list would be extremely beneficial.**

As you will notice in this book, I always try to focus on things you can do to prove your worth before even stepping inside the interview room and to prep you for solid developer habits to aid you in your daily tasks.

III

CV

*Tips and tricks for CV optimization.
It is a very standardized piece of digital paper, that
most of the time, you pay not enough attention to.
That piece of paper is your **first impression**, so let's
make sure it's good.*

7

Styling

It pains me to even think about writing or updating a CV. It's a hassle that feels incredibly uninspiring. I wish I had some tricks to make this process enjoyable, but unfortunately, I don't. If you happen to have any, please reach out and let me know.

What to remove

When it comes to your CV, avoid starting with your **personal history**. Details like your lower education, birthday, or enthusiasm to work with the company are not crucial for the job and are often considered as given facts.

Consider removing these details from your CV altogether, or if you feel they might spark extra a bit of extra curiosity, place them at the very end.

It's up to you to determine which parts are crucial. However, for each piece of information, ask yourself if

41

it will help you secure the job. You must be **strict** and leave only the most **succinct pieces of information**.

What to emphasize

When writing, start with a clear reason why you're a perfect fit. Your first sentence should be your **strongest selling point**. Skip the pleasantries like "Hi!" or "I really love what you're doing" and get straight to the point. For example, you might say:

"I am confident that my strong work ethic will compensate for my lack of experience."

In that simple intro sentence you addressed one of the biggest pain-points for them, in case you are a junior with no experience.

You might go further and shorten that to:

"My strong work ethic will compensate for my lack of experience."

Read and re-write to make it clearer, remove **extra wording**, "**sharpen**" it until it is as clear as possible and easy to read.

When someone reads your CV, remember that they are your **friend** and genuinely want the best for you. They aren't searching for holes in your experience; instead, they are seeking reasons to invite you for an interview. **Your task is simply to provide them with those reasons.**

To achieve that, prioritize saving their time as much as you can.

Continue with any relevant work experience and, if possible, add a personal touch to make it **stand out**.

What to avoid

I've witnessed this far too often: mindlessly **listing technologies** and **frameworks** just to have them present on the page. But here's the thing, if you mention more than three technologies all in one line, you lose the reader. It becomes a meaningless string of words that they **skim over**. I get it, you want to showcase your skills, but please, wrap it in a story. Turn it into a paragraph, anything except a mundane list.

This issue often arises after listing a project you've worked on, followed by a **jumble** of technologies separated only by commas. Just because it's a CV doesn't mean it has to be dull. In fact, I even have an actual joke in mine.

What to present

When it comes to that joke, I've had several people ask me: "What if a company sees that as unprofessional and decides not to invite you?"

It's a legitimate question and **makes sense**. But do you really want to work for a company that is so strict about a simple joke in your CV? After all, your CV represents you, **not the company**.

So, to answer the question, I would say, "Yes, it does matter, and I don't want to work for those companies in the first place."

Essentially, the joke in my CV serves as a **filter**, a way for me to test the company's culture and values because I am also choosing a good fit for myself.

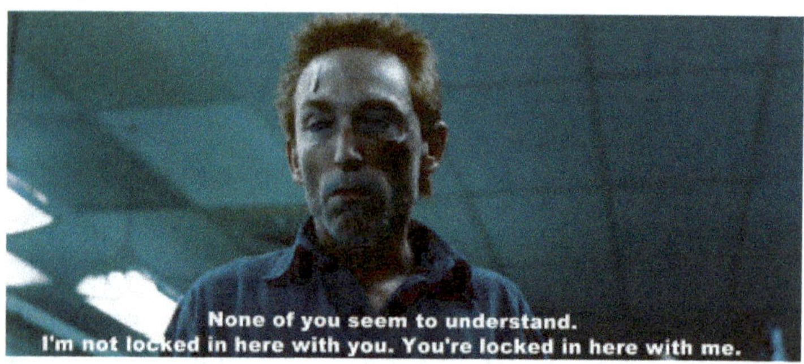

Therefore, make sure to showcase not just your **qualifications**, but also your **character** and **soft skills**. If you strip away all personality from your resume, can you really blame recruiters for viewing you as just **another number?**

> *When writing a CV, make sure your personality show but remain professional. Do not crack jokes on each paragraph but do not be afraid to let your human side* ***leave some trace*** *either.*

With all of this applied, your CV should be clean and focused, aligning perfectly with their requirements. **Next, let's talk design.**

8

Design

Despite having over a decade of design experience, I still find this step challenging. It is not because I don't know how to do it, but rather because there are far **too many possibilities** for what can be done with it.

No Colors (I am lying)

If possible, limit the number of colors in your CV. Printing is not the main reason to avoid colors, as most people won't print it anyway, but rather because they don't add much value.

You can use color sparingly for headers or accents, but be cautious about it.

To be honest, my own CV does have a color element, but it was created a few years ago. Now, I think using a clean black would work better. Here's a quick preview.

If you do decide to use a color, make sure it is a darker shade. Orange/yellow and light blue are out of the question for example. Contrast is rather poor with those colors, and are usually used for other purposes. Orange/yellow for food related themes for example.

I believe it goes without saying that having a background other then white is **out of the question** for obvious reasons.

Fonts

When it comes to fonts, it's best not to experiment too much. Keep it simple by using either a default font or one that closely resembles it. Serif fonts are also fine; personally, I've been leaning towards them lately, but that might just be a sign of me getting older.

Regardless of the font you choose, define **three styles** and stick to them. Have one main headline style for sections, one middle-sized style (which can be bold), and one style for content text.

I've noticed people using multiple font variants, and it can really disrupt the layout of a well-designed CV. While it may look visually appealing for a single section, when someone quickly scans through the document, it's important to ensure a **smooth**

flow.

Photo

While some companies may require you to omit a photo from your CV, I personally believe in **including one**. Although having a photo may not necessarily improve your chances of getting a job, I find the concept of removing all individuality from a CV **nonsensical** (now that is a grown up word right there :). I would rather **defy** this notion than conform to it.

However, if you prefer not to include a photo, that is entirely up to you and perfectly ok. With everything I mention here, it is still your CV that **represents you**. My opinion is still just that, an opinion. I am, however, always interested in discussing anything that you might disagree with. (@ me on twitter)

Contact Info

You do not need all possible links in there, but list of the ones that are **almost required** are:

- Phone
- Email
- Linkedin
- GitHub (if you are a developer)

Anything beyond that is considered **noise**, particularly since this list is already lengthy.

Ensure that the items in the list are **linkable** and that the links actually work. This way, if someone wants to quickly take a look at your LinkedIn profile, they can do so without much hassle. Copy-pasting may not be a lot of work, but if you have to do it all the time, it becomes cumbersome.

Format

PDF, PDF and only PDF. Compress it, make it small, and that's it. Do not ZIP it, do not send a WordDoc variant. Act as if there is nothing else out there besides PDF, because there isn't, and there **never should be**.

9

Cover Letter

This information can either be included in your CV or sent as a **separate document**.

Whether it should be sent separately depends on the instructions provided, but personally, I prefer to include it as **part of the CV**. This approach reduces friction since it eliminates the need to open two separate files, making the process **more efficient**.

1<2, be careful with all this advanced knowledge I am giving you.

Content

When writing a letter, it is not a **groundbreaking** advice to suggest researching the company and their past endeavors. However, try to do more than simply mentioning a few of their projects. Instead, take the time to do a quick Google search, read blogs, and explore their website.

Then, focus on a **single aspect** of the app and dig into why you liked it. You can ask questions about why they chose a specific approach or even suggest alternatives, but generally just ask a few meaningful questions about it to get the conversation going.

Another important consideration is the **length of the letter**. While there are no strict rules, I personally recommend keeping it within three paragraphs. The first paragraph serves as an **introduction**, the second should pertain to **their company and position**, and the third can be used to **sign off**.

Each paragraph can be around 150 words, but the first and last paragraphs are typically shorter. Remember, this layout is just a **preference** and not a hard rule.

> *Your cover letter content should be very on point and clear. Look at it as a short email which should be read withing 1 minute.*
>
> *Mention yourself, position and the company through-out.*

10

App Section

If you're an iOS developer, chances are you have **apps** that you've either created or worked on. However, when it comes to writing a CV, it can be **challenging** to present them effectively.

Simply including a link in your document and expecting hiring managers to visit the app store and download the app is asking for a lot, especially when they have **numerous candidates** to consider. This is even more problematic if your app requires a login or has a lengthy **on-boarding** process that would take more than a few minutes to go through.

A no-no

On the off-chance that you're sharing links to your GitHub projects, **yiiikes**! If someone is willing to do that, it means they already want you, and consider you hired in their mind, so seems a giant overkill. On the other side of things it will frighten the non-tech folk. Link to your Github profile is fine, but not the repo.

The do-do's

As with many of the steps mentioned earlier, our goal is to **reduce friction** as much as possible. Below are several ways to achieve that. You can choose one approach, combine them, or use something new that really works for you. Remember, **this CV is you.**

MVP

The first thing you need to do, is to add an icon in your PDF and a link to the material posted on your preferred video hosting platform. You can choose to have 2 links per item, one for the demo and one for the AppStore link, but in my experience demo is chosen by the majority or recruiters.

Here's a quick example from my own (though rather outdated) CV.

Quick Video Demo

The first approach is to record your screen while using the app. Choose a path that is the most enjoyable to follow. Your app may have many screens or offer various user experiences, but try to keep it simple and time-efficient.

The video should not exceed 3 minutes in length, ideally 1-2 minutes. Avoid adding music, voice-overs, or any additional elements. Just record your screen as you navigate through the app's best features.

The reason for avoiding the audio is that no one likes an unexpected cheap explainer music in the middle of their carefully crafted playlist for the day.

Music is to be added and present only when expected.

Guided Demo

Similar to the previous approach, this method requires more effort to record and present.

Here's how it works: set up a camera focused on you, providing occasional context for the screen being presented. During the presentation, switch the camera view from you to the screen and back.

This approach allows for a more personal touch and emphasizes the details within the app. It also allows for a longer duration of the presentation.

Identify interesting parts of the app where you anticipate the most questions. A presentation of this size can help users learn more about the app and address any burning questions they may have. And remember, make it enjoyable when all is said and done.

Technical Demo

If your app is complex or involves a highly technical approach, you might want to consider creating a keynote presentation. This presentation could include code snippets and video demos, recorded as if you were giving a live demo to an audience.

This approach works best for showcasing the backend development of the app, which may be difficult to fully understand from the frontend presentation alone. While this technique is typically reserved for more complex projects, it can also be applied to simpler apps. I wouldn't necessarily recommend it for every situation, but starting with a video demo and then diving into the code allows viewers to stop at any point. Even those who aren't proficient in coding may appreciate the extra effort.

Audio/Video

Whichever method you choose, it is paramount to ensure that the audio quality is as good as possible. While it may not be easy to invest in professional equipment or change the appearance of your room, the attention you give to audio will pay off in the long run.

When it comes to audio, consider testing whether it's better to record on your Mac, iPhone, or even with an external microphone.

For video, a screen recorder can come to your rescue, but be mindful of your background and any potential noise.

Some may view this as over-engineering, but there's nothing worse than opening a video and struggling to hear the presenter, or encountering loud, distracting noises from the speakers.

Alternatives

There might be a myriad of reasons why you are not sure about recording a demo. Your equipment might be sub-par, or you are an introverted person, not ready to put themselves out there in this way. I hear you, you are not alone in this.

Fortunately, in today's digital age, nearly every problem can be solved with online assistance. While I haven't personally used Fiverr for this purpose, it seems like a great use-case for the platform. You can record the video portion and seamlessly add professional audio on top of it, effectively resolving the issue.

Alternatively, you could ask a friend who is less audio-shy to help you out. The main objective is to convey your message clearly, so any approach that achieves that is worth considering. Just be cautious about using generic upbeat explainer video music, as it may hinder your chances of landing the job instead of helping you.

> Presenting your work in a friction-less manner is crucial to give yourself a fighting chance. Including video demos in your CV is something that will undoubtedly capture the attention of any hiring manager. At the very least, they will appreciate the effort.

11

Interview

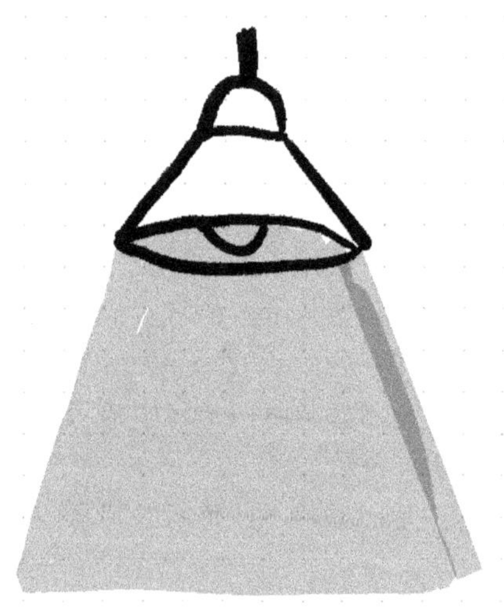

Although this section is focused on the CV (written part), hopefully your in person interview would swiftly follow and more importantly, it also affects how you record the videos for apps. For those reasons I thought it earned its place here.

It can be the most stressful and gut wrenching experience, while also being on of the most humbling and memorable ones in your life. You are put on "stage" of sorts, all lights are on you and you need to look....professional?? Yeah, can be quite tricky!

The more interviews that you do, the easier it becomes, but it never gets so easy to the point where you can be fully relaxed unfortunately.

I was always fairy ok with them to start with, and now looking back and analyzing why that is, few things come to mind. Primarily, I am a military kid. My father has been in the army literally since he finished primary school, and that is where he met my mom as well...so, you do the math.

My parents were never too strict on how my sister and I acted or dressed, they allowed us to be creative and well...kids!

Few things that they instilled in us were:

- punctuality (we always ate lunch at 15h)
- information sharing (skip lunch or move it, but inform ahead of time)
- eye-contact when meeting or talking with someone
- firm(but not too firm) of a handshake
- talk clearly and pause if necessary
- ...along with other life lessons of course, but I picked ones that can be used for this environment

Talk

That last point in the last section is incredibly important. When you are being interviewed, you have to be **heard**. Make sure to talk loud enough and with conviction. If you are afraid to say something incorrectly, well, talking quiet will not stop you from being wrong isn't it?

Another thing I my father was very clear about is to put emphasis on how important it is to remove the "uhms" and "ahms". When asked a question, take a few seconds to construct your answer, and then talk. If you are lost in your thought and need to recollect, just stop and think instead of inserting the "uhmmm" in between. You would be amazed how much it affects your delivery.

Smile

Sure, sounds almost too easy and evident! "Droping some real gold nuggets here Emin!"

But remembering this can be harder than just thinking about it. It the moment we are already trying not to be wrong and to concentrate on the task/topic, it is so easy to become too serious and to lose that "relaxed" vibe.

Do not smile ALL the time or if it is not natural. A smile here and there where it feels right is a good measure, especially if it is accompanied by eye-contact.

What you are trying to do here is to simply create and maintain positive environment throughout the interview.

Posture

Another thing that can affect your impression is how you sit/stand. We can easily go into that regular "slouched" position as the conversation drags on. Maintaining proper posture gives you a good base and ensures you look engaged, along with sounding like it too. Whatever your natural position to sit in is, go for it, as long as it is professional enough depending on the environment.

Practice

With these three elements combined, you will appear more friendly, easy to talk to and professional. However, when it comes to working on these things, it is naive to think that you can only "try your best" when the issue arises, and if you think they are simple concepts anyone can master, you are sorely mistaken.

Don't forget that I am not listing these points as some random ideas of mine, but something that has surfaced after years of being on both sides of the interviewing table, from colleagues with similar experience, books and blogs. It all seems so easy and straightforward, but I dare you to try this next exercise and prove me wrong.

Test

I mentioned before that I will not try to point to specific resources as not to make the book feel like and ad, but when there is a resource that absolutely blows me away, I simply have to share it here. If you search for **@askvinh** on YouTube, you will find large number of short videos, most of them containing gold nuggets of knowledge and tips on how to present yourself vocally.

One thing that has stuck with me for months now is his suggestion on how to improve your public speaking skills. It starts with making a video recording of yourself talking about a specific subject. Then, go over that video in 3 stages:

- mute the audio and just watch yourself
- close your eyes and only listen
- repeat (focusing on improving one of those points)

The idea is that only by only **watching** yourself you will pay attention to how you gesticulate. If you smile, what your posture is and similar. In the second step, if you only **listen** to yourself, you will be only focusing on your pronunciation and the speed that you're talking etc.

To verify how effective this is, I do recommend that you pick a certain subject that you know the most about, or you can imagine that you're applying for a certain position at XYZ company, and just give it a quick go. Record a video of one minute or two and then look at it, and see what is missing. Try to be fully immersive with the whole approach and then perform the test listed above.

I absolutely guarantee that after three or four repetitions your demeanor will improve by a certain factor.

Most of us believe that it is easy to pay attention on how we present ourselves and just do it on the spot when needed. It is **only** improved by literally practicing in front of the mirror or in front of the camera. Almost exactly like in Sims That is the only way to move forward!

Interview checklist

```
[ ] - Talk Clearly
[ ] - Smile occasionally
[ ] - Mind your posture
[ ] - Practise
[ ] - Test
[ ] - Repeat
```

12

Unsolicited advice

I keep going back and forth on whether to add this to the book, and already a few times was ready to hit the "publish" button, but I felt guilty not sharing everything that I can. After all, this book if about helping people get jobs, and when I asked myself "Will this help people get jobs?", the answer was unequivocal yes. Therefore, in the book it goes!

Jitters

Imagine this:

> *Standing in front of the big crowd, you try to speak, and Alvin the Chipmunk comes out.*

Sound familiar? If not, consider yourself lucky! Good number of people tend to treble in front of a big crowd. Worst thing about it is that you are not really aware of it or have control over it. In my case, I feel no stress in general, but my breathing is way too shallow and I cannot help but get a shaky voice. By the end of the talk it tends to get better, but the longer its there, the more subconscious you become. A downward spiral that just keeps going.

I was always confused how uncontrollable it is, until I read an advice about it from Vinh Giang.

> The secret? **Do PUSHUPS!**
> Shaking is caused by surge of adrenaline due to high stress, but you as are standing still, your body has no choice but to tremble. It needs to use that adrenaline somehow, so by doing exercises before the talk or moving on the stage quickly, your muscles will have other things to do then to tremble. (pushups are just one example, any quick movement would help)

Imagine your body was an engine, it would be as if you are standing in neutral but have your foot fully on the throttle. Surely not a good sound for extended period of time.

Dress Code

I am all for freedom in everything we do, how we dress, how we look etc...But in the scenario where you are trying to present yourself in the best possible light when first meeting someone, you need to play all the cards right.

Here is the tricky part tho, you cannot overdo it. If you do not wear suits but suddenly decide to do it for the interview, it will show. Either the size would be wrong or you will just not be used to it. And all those little detail tend to be visible.

Stay true to your style and how you usually dress, but try to push it one level higher. Clean and tidy, your favorite shirt, everything ironed out etc.

For the fellas, you have to make sure to be clean shaven or that your beard is "up to code" and not unruly.

Camera Mode

Lately, home office has become the standard in the tech industry, and with it, online meetings instead of in-person ones are now common. Same as for the previous section applies, but try to pay attention to the quality of your video and you look on the camera.

Ensuring audio is clean is a paramount and do try to get some proper lighting. I am not saying to get full professional video gear and lighting, but it is so easy to reconsider where in your house do you want to seat, and ensuring audio quality is up to par.

Whatever the setup, and your capabilities, try to make sure to maximize the quality and visuals.

You would be surprised how little effort would improve your chances greatly. First impressions matter, there is no way around it.

> *Just to give you an idea how you could "manage":*
>
> *Once for an interview I had a such a bad setup, that i ended up using my 3 year old's stool, with an old phone pointing a flashlight at the wall to get some semi-natural light on my face. They had one idea, but my video was on point. I think they even mentioned that.*

Ask them to twist the knife

Yes, you might and will get rejected, it just the way in goes. But try to capitalist on that opportunity and ask for the reasons why. If you are lucky, they would be brutally honest and tell you why it did not work out. Which is always good for you, it is something you can work on for your next interview! Not a win but a good consolation prize.

Connect-Reconnect

Often times, there will be issues with communication. Make sure to send a "see you soon" email a day or two before your interview, it will clear up any possible issues in communication and helps build rapport. You do not have to literally check "are we still on", but you might say that you are looking forward to have a chat and that they can let you know if you need to prep anything on your end for the interview.

Similarly, after you had a chat, send a follow-up email, thanking for the opportunity and acknowledging you had a good time. In the follow up you might want to emphasize how any answer, good or bad, might be helpful and appreciated. This way you HOPEFULLY increase your chances of getting a straight answer. Unfortunately, companies have a habit of only contacting the candidates that went through, making it even worse for others who never got "closure". Trying to eliminate this would allow you to move faster, and learn what you need to improve upon.

IV

Junior Dev Checklist

Since I began my journey in iOS development, I have always been uncertain about where the line is drawn between a junior developer and a medior/senior developer. People often told me that the separation is not clearly defined, but I was determined to prove them wrong someday.

After years of experience, I finally discovered the secret:
the separation is not that clear-cut.

13

Dev Checklist

Although the lines are not always clear, junior positions do have certain, very strictly defined concepts which you are expected to know about.

The following list includes those concepts that both myself and those around me have identified as a "must have".

It is by no means exhaustive, but rather a compilation of glaring issues most devs would consider a red flag if they are not familiar to you.

If you feel something is missing from this list, please feel free to reach out to me directly on X (@emin_ui).

```
[ ] - Networking
[ ] - Auth
[ ] - JSON
[ ] - Git
[ ] - Storage (UserDefaults/CoreData)
[ ] - Closures
[ ] - Debugging
```

14

Networking

This is THE red flag to be weary of, and you might as well say it: "You will never get hired if you are not familiar networking."

Luckily, I am also sure that chances of you not coming across this are extremely slim, and would be astonished if you have NOT come into contact with networking by now. It is a backbone of everything we do and frankly, not sure I ever saw or worked on an app that does not have a tiny bit of networking.

This is after all, a checklist, and we need to have "things to check", so let's actually do that.

Basic Networking

Know how to write code to actually make a network call. You are expected to know about **URLSession** and how to create a simple call by either using **completion handlers** or **async/await**. The later is definitely more relatable these days, but working with completion handlers is still required in 2023, so keep that in mind.

Forget about ~~combine~~ as it was a promising tech which got destroyed by async/await simplicity. Sure, it is still present and some use it, but you will not be looked down at for not knowing anything about it. Truth be told, even people who wrote combine code probably forgot about it already.

Anatomy of a URLRequest

To make any network call you need to know about **types of calls** (GET, POST, UPDATE, DELETE...), ways a **body** is constructed, and of course **headers!** Some APIs require you send your data as URLQuery parameters, while others to encode the body of the HTML request with the JSON data. To cover most of these I would simply recommend searching for "Swift networking simple API" or similar, and just go over several approaches, see which one works best for you.

Be aware, this is not a quick 30 minute tutorial you need to go over and be done with it. Take your time, understand how it works, so down the line you can pick and choose in which way to solve a particular issue or adapt to the client API.

Just to help you in your quest, I will post a very small example I did just now, for presentation purposes.

```swift
struct BookTestAPI {

  struct Endpoint {
    let path: String
    let queryItems: [URLQueryItem]
    let apiVersion: String = "/rest/v1"
```

```swift
  var url: URL? {
    var components = URLComponents()
    components.scheme = "https"
    components.host = "testdomain.com"
    components.path = apiVersion + path
    components.queryItems = queryItems
    return components.url
  }
}


 struct Request {
  enum Path: String {
   case firstEndpoint = "/testbookendpoint"
  }

  static func testRequest(with path: Path,
  customQuery: [URLQueryItem] = []) -> URLRequest? {

   var queryItems = customQuery
   queryItems.append(URLQueryItem(name: "select",
   value: "*"))

   guard let url = Endpoint(
    path: path.rawValue,
    queryItems: queryItems
   ).url else { return nil }

   var request = URLRequest(url: url)
   return request
  }
 }
}


//When used, you would call it as such:
let request: URLRequest =
BookTestAPI.testRequest(with: .firstEndpoint)
```

Headers

Although mentioned as a part of the anatomy, headers are extremely important so they deserve a separate mention as well. Headers are usually always used to define the content-type, but more importantly to carry the authorization info. There is not a LOT to say about them specifically, basically it's just another value that is set on your URLRequest, but the most important value of all. So, read up on their history and usage, but to give you a quick example usage here is some code:

```swift
extension URLRequest {
  mutating func addAuthHeader() {
    self.setValue("<SUPER-SECRET-KEY>",
    forHTTPHeaderField: "Authorization")
  }
}
```

See? Simple as can be, but how you supply that secret key and carry it around will be a real detail to focus on. Not something we can cover in this book, but also not something you need to worry about just yet.

The fact that you know how these values are added to the request (as in the code example) is pretty much enough for any team to go on. There will surely be a more senior developer to handle the security of the secret key.

15

Authorization

Tokens

Tokens are secret strings generated during the initial "hand-shake" with the backend. These tokens act as your pass to access additional information from the server without requiring re-authorization.

Access Token

The primary token you commonly receive during the login net-work call. It is simply attached to all, or most requests through the header. The standard key for this header is "Authorization," but it can be something else if defined by the backend.

An access token has a limited validity duration and will expire in about an hour, or longer, as defined by the backend, after which you need to obtain the next token. This is where the refresh token comes into play.

Refresh Token

Refresh token is valid for a lot longer than the access token, sometimes a week, or a month. It can however, be revoked after a single use, depending on your setup.

As the sole purpose of a refresh token is to get another access token, it is to be used when the access token expires. There are different approaches to this mechanism, I will describe 2 which I have come across so far.

Pre-refresh

When you receive the access token, note the duration of its validity and set the date of expiry. Then, as user nears the expiry date, send a refresh token in the background and perform a refresh. This approach is fun to work with, but very rarely used.

Post-refresh

More commonly used method, and one that is required in the previous usage as well, is simply to use the access token until the backend informs you of its expiry. Then, refresh the token, and repeat the request that initially got the expiry response.

This covers the essential information for authorization, which also involves networking knowledge, but there are some caveats.

As a junior developer, you won't be required to create an entirely foolproof authentication solution, so don't worry. There will likely be senior developers available to assist with this. Your role will be to support them by understanding the process and the overall setup.

16

JSON Decoding

Networking can lose its value if you struggle with interpreting the data obtained from the backend. JSON decoding transforms raw data into meaningful objects for app use.

Fortunately, in Swift, this process has become straightforward, no longer viewed as a separate skill. While complexities may arise occasionally, it mostly involves aligning expected and received data.

Although tools exist to auto-generate complete Swift models from JSON, I recommend crafting your own structs manually. While leveraging available tools is usually beneficial, relying on them here is akin to using a calculator before learning basic arithmetic. This manual approach allows you to refine your skills, as pre-generated templates may not always be optimal.

There is not much depth to JSON decoding, but exactly because of that, and the fact that it is an integral part of any app, is seen as an absolute no-no if you fail to have proper familiarity with it.

17

GIT

GitHub / Gitlab etc..

It is doubtful that you will be asked anything about GitHub, even for the most junior of positions. It is expected that you are fairly familiar with some version control system and that you actively use it. You are not expected to be using rebase on a regular basis or that your merge-conflict handling it off the charts. Push-pull-branching and making a PR is all you need to be "usable". Over time you will gain more familiarity when working in a big team and how they operate.

> One crucial question you have to ask is: **What is your git workflow from getting a ticket to merging?**

This process is never complex and fairly straightforward, but by going through the whole process you will build confidence not to f*&k something up when making you very first PR.

First PR

No matter your level of experience, the first PRs are tough! When you're opening your code to a new group, it's natural to feel extra cautious and self-conscious. Here are a few tips:

- Start with a small task; it's actually preferred by the team.
- Avoid overthinking and making it overly detailed; work as you normally would.
- Double-check for any spelling errors.
- Provide a detailed explanation of the PR and don't rush for approvals.
- Using a label if applicable (and used in the project)

As time goes on, it will become easier based on your skills and team communication. Just remember, feeling this way about your first PR is completely normal. We've all been there.

Tools

If you're a terminal user, that's great. If you prefer GitHub Desktop, fantastic. Kraken? Excellent!

The truth is, there are no bad tools, only poor usage. I used to think using the terminal made me look more "professional," but I learned it doesn't matter as long as the work gets done well. So, use whatever tool feels right for you.

I recommend exploring other solutions whenever possible. There are numerous fantastic apps available, and depending on your needs, you might transition from simpler tools to more sophisticated ones. Personally, I prefer GitHub Desktop for its simplicity because, at heart, I'm a simple person.

Resolving conflicts

When working alone, it is really hard to learn about something that is fairly impossible to create, merge conflicts! they sound scary, and can be, but most of the time is just choosing the door A, B or something in between.

However, to not be afraid of them you need to experience some common merge conflicts on your own, somehow. It can be as easy as merging one branch that holds a similar change prior to merging the branch #2, only to receive a conflicts. It is at this point that your tool of choice becomes important and with some experimentation you will find which one works best for you.

> There is a good chance that all of this is quite common to you and you are wondering why am I even mentioning it? I am doing that for that small percentage of people who are not that familiar using GIT and who absolutely have to be ready for it on their first job. I will also stress that you do not need to be a git pro, just to know how it works.

18

Storage

UserDefaults / CoreData

Most apps will eventually require data storage. Initially, you may use UserDefaults for its simplicity, but when a more robust solution is needed, CoreData or an external SPM package becomes necessary.

Understanding when to choose one over the other is crucial. For CoreData, familiarity with CRUD operations (create/read/update/delete) is essential. Knowledge of Realm or GRDB can be a valuable asset for junior developers. The mere mention of something other than CoreData for an entry level job would definitely turn some heads.

Working with complex objects in CoreData may seem intimidating, but mastering this skill can significantly enhance your job prospects and make you a more valuable team member, increasing your chances of being hired. Not something you

HAVE TO master, but it could be an easy win on your side.

So, try to cover as much as you can and ask around for some basic data structures. Take inspiration from some of the apps you use. If you listen to music, you know artist has multiple albums which in turn have multiple tracks etc... Ensure that data gets stored and read properly and you are already good enough for more app use cases.

> It is easy to think knowledge about these concepts is enough, but knowing how to use them, is something far more valuable to your perspective employer. Explaining the reasoning how you would approach the data storage is crucial.

19

Closures

Closures and completion handlers are essential components of any codebase. Some might argue that it's impossible to have a functional app without them.

I recall struggling with this topic, revisiting tutorials multiple times before it finally clicked. Certain concepts require repeated exposure to fully grasp. While I can't quite put my finger on why it was challenging initially, I now recognize that they may seem perplexing at first glance.

I do encourage you to explore some more complex examples of closures. This will help broaden your horizons and deepen your understanding of the context. After those "regular everyday" closures become ez-pz-lemon-squezzy.

To be a tad more specific, ensure you car write a method which utilizes closures. Using existing methods is easier, but writing a method from scratch is a different beast. I specifically remember taking this for granted and then stopped to thing

WHERE do I exactly write the @escaping.

You just thought about it and are not 100% sure, right?

20

Debugging

Often overlooked, the real challenge boils down to one question: "Can you find this screen in the code?"

Seems straightforward, doesn't it? However, with certain architectures, this task can be quite tricky, especially if you're not familiar with the setup or data flow. Reused views, lengthy view model names, and similar factors can easily lead you astray, sending you searching for a screen in the wrong place.

Starting in an unfamiliar codebase with limited experience requires you to identify a starting point and follow through until you unravel the entire thread. At times, you may have no other choice but to persist in this manner.

It's crucial to develop and utilize tactics that are quick to implement. Don't hesitate to add print statements for debugging, set breakpoints on various screens, or strategically use fatalError() to verify if a specific screen is being accessed. Remember, at this stage, your motto should be "if it works, it's not broken."

While it does become easier over time, I must admit that even now, I still struggle at times to navigate through files and pinpoint the correct screen in the code. Don't pressure yourself into thinking that this task should always be effortless.

Print()

One of the simplest and, in my opinion, most effective methods of debugging to this day is using a straightforward print() call when needed. It provides real-time information about the app's flow and values. Setting a breakpoint can sometimes lag, while print() is executed as soon as it's reached. Simple and efficient.

> **Tip#1:** When adding a print statement, get into a habit of prefixing it with something like "<YOUR_NAME>:" that way, when the time comes to cleanup, a simple search will do the trick.

> **Tip#2:** Add an appropriate emoji to your print statement, it will help you locate the print in a sea of debug logs.

LLDB

An extremely valuable debugging method which comes in handy when you face complex issues that simple print statements cannot resolve. In case you're unfamiliar with it, setting a breakpoint allows the app to halt execution, granting you access to the lldb debugger in your console. From there, you can enter commands like:

```
po <myVar>
```

The PO command will replace your print statement and can be called multiple times. You can even write a whole method for it to execute, although doing so in one line would be quite tricky.

While there are other commands available, PO is the most commonly used one in my opinion. Understanding this will definitely help you make significant progress in digging deeper.

> Main takeaway is to try and develop strategies in locating issues in code. Ask your fellow devs which approach they prefer and why, and then start using what works best for you.

21

«Add item here»

This is where your research comes in. The items listed above are basic concepts that emerged from conversations with close friends and colleagues. You can do the same. You likely know someone in the industry or have an online presence you can leverage to gather additional information and refine the checklist.

A straightforward question to ask is:

> "If you were to interview me for the X position, which question would determine if I am being hired or not?"

or a slight variation:

> "If you were to interview me for the X position, which concept would make you want to stop the interview and show me the door?"

It is really important to have a clearly defined question, so make sure to think about what you want to ask carefully. Upon asking it, keep quiet and wait for them to think about it a bit. Reason why this is important, is that you are trying to really put them in the shoes of a hiring manager, and not your friend who wishes you well already. Even better if you can ask this question a complete stranger.

V

Assignments

This chapter covers various types of interviewing setups and hiring practices. Unfortunately, it appears that they are deteriorating year over year, so my commentary in this chapter might come across as more critical. Apologies in advance.

22

Algorithmic assignments

I'm not sure when or where this trend started, but it seems to have originated from the biggest companies in Silicon Valley and unfortunately, it caught on. Smaller companies also began adopting this practice, often without fully understanding why, other than the fact that "the big players are doing it."

I can see why large corporations would implement this approach – they face a high volume of daily applicants and need a rigorous screening process to identify candidates with strong problem-solving skills.

Even though algorithmic questions may not directly relate to our day-to-day tasks, for these companies, the goal is to filter out candidates who have undergone specific training and endured hours of whiteboard challenges. And for them, this method simply works.

For smaller companies, this practice may seem like shooting themselves in the foot. These companies often receive just a couple of applicants per day, yet they continue to use algorithm tests. Why? Because candidates keep taking them, and this trend is likely to persist.

It is unfortunate that most of these questions are FUN to solve. As developers, we are naturally inclined to tackle challenges and find solutions. But seing them used in an interview environment kind kills the fun and transforms them into nightmares. Moreover, having specific problems to practice and prepare for simplifies the process, unlike the uncertainty of guessing what might be asked.

As you can tell, I am very much against these types of interviews (although I love me a puzzle), and I have been lucky enough not to interact with companies that do ask for algo questions. I also reached the level of being able to tell the company "No, I will not do this", due to having a job already and hiring history, allowing for more negotiations tactics.

I know looking for the first job is already hard enough, you cannot put this blocker there as well, making things even harder. If you still want to do it, I applaud you. But if you cannot skip this, it is very understandable.

All you can do, is to genuinely prepare for this, but do keep few things in mind:

- it is not really about reaching the "correct" answer
- do not rush or stress too much, they are simply assessing your thinking process
- ask as much as you can, these assignments are not meant to be solved in silence
- if confused, tell them so, they want to give you hints and guide you

- try to take a step back and tell them, "give me a minute to think about this"
- talk them through your thinking. If you say something wrong but then correct yourself is a **LOT** better then just showing the correct answer.

When doing these assignments it is **VERY** hard to keep a cool head, and any interviewer knows this. For this reason they will always give you some leniency when solving it. In most cases interviewers already have solved variant in front of them and they want you to succeed. What is important, is to communicate with the interviewer as much as you can, and keep that rhythm throughout the process. They literally want to hear your train of thought and to see if that makes sense. It can be wrong, but then again some of these assignments are almost meant to push you down the wrong path, just to see how you recover.

So if at all possible try to forgive yourself some mistakes, as you are meant to make them.

> *Biggest takeaway for algorithmic assignments is to try to find your comfort zone and believe that right answers are not what will get you to the other side. That, and practice them as much as you can...sorry about that.*

23

Take-home assignment

Take home assignments are rather common lately and personally I would prefer them to other approaches any day of the week.
They allow for quick insight into your coding style, while not
stressing the applicant more than required. They are usually
not timed and you do them at you own convenience, so its rather
easy to find time to do them if you are employed or have do not
have as much free time during the day.

It depends on the company, but usually the scope it not big,
as not to take too much of your time, but if you are not careful
this can actually trip you. More on that later.

The Scope

While you might get a checklist of things needed in the app,
you will definitely feel inclined to do a bit more on top of that,
especially if you want to leave a good impression. However,
depending on the company this could be your downfall, as it
might be looked down upon to to a lot more than required,
therefore proving that you worked more hours than it was

meant to be allocated for this, and that you are poor in following instructions.

You need to do EXACTLY what was asked of you, and keep your own checklist of completed sections, for reference. Far be it from being disallowed to add anything on top of it, but if you do decide to do that, make sure it is not substantial and that it really makes sense to be there. For example, they might not ask of you to add error handling, but simple addition of an alert that pops up saying "Something went wrong" will surely buy you some points.

Timing

You need to hit the goldilocks zone here. Not too fast but do not wait for the last day. If they say the limit is 5 days, send it on the 4th. If however you realize you might not make it by day 5, ask for an extension as soon as you can, maybe even on day 2 is you saw your weekly obligations and realized you will not make it in time.

Take-home tests are **not made** only to test how well you can make the app, but how you assess the time given and how much you plan ahead. If you keep a journal of your changes and record the whole process, even better.

Design

Design is never really mentioned or taken into consideration on paper, but it is impossible for us to see something that looks good and stay indifferent to it. No matter how much they say in the assignment not to pay any attention to it, you really should. A good icon and a nice color scheme will not hurt anyone, and it is bound to help you rank higher if only for the "looks".

No worries if you are not really design savvy. Just go on dribbble.com, find an app that you like with a neat graphics and copy as much as you can. No one will judge you for it, yet everyone will appreciate the extra effort. Best thing about it is that it cannot be looked down upon as it not a part of the assignment in the first place, so it can only help you.

Tech

One thing to consider when coding the actual assignment is not to feel constrained to the task itself. You should always think about scalability of the project and how this would be used in a real-life environment if only it was expanded from. As most of these projects are 10% of a real app, pretended that someone else will do the other 90% and prepare your code for it.

Add comments and explanations where needed, but do not riddle your code with comments for each line.

Clean up all the prints and unnecessary code, use a linter to make it nicely formatted and easy to read.

> *Developers looking over this code might be tied into an OS which is few steps behind the latest one, but are hungry for new tech and new toys which they cannot play with, but you can! Show them the latest toys which will surely spur more interesting questions and discussions later on.*

24

Code Analysis

Less seen in the "wild", but some companies prefer to see some of your existing code. They would ask you to forward a project or two that you find interesting for them to analyze and assess your quality as a developer.

Let's just forget about the fact that we are all subconscious and don't like anyone looking at our code. That is a given and takes quite some time before one is ready to freely share the code they have written. It is something unavoidable so best get used to it soon.

What to send?

This will be specified by the hiring manager, but they usually ask for something you deem interesting and that you are proud of. I know, it's hard to be fully proud of the code we have written as only few days later we already look at it in shame. Especially when first starting out, your progress will be so much faster, that week-over-week you will keep finding issues in the code you have written previously.

Be that as it may, your code needs to be analyzed and any reviewer would take into account your experience and some possible mistakes.

You would then need to pick something that you had fun working on, and what possibly could spur some discussions with the reviewers. Maybe you did something a tad unconventional and want to challenge the standard way of doing things? Or maybe it was extremely hard to solve and you wanted to make the effort worth it by using that code to show off your skills?

Do not be afraid to send a simple extension you did for a type. It does not need to be a part of the app or a whole app at all. It can be a module you worked on or a nice decoder helper for JSON!

> *Whatever it is, the more personal the better. Do not ask yourself "what do they want to see?", but " what do I want to show?"*

How many?

There is definitely a limit as to how many examples you should send. Too many and they will not know what to pick, too few and it seems you don't have a lot to show.

If not defined by them, 2–3 examples is quite a good number. Use 2 if they are a bit heavy on the amount of code, or 3 if you are presenting smaller snippets.

Usually there is not a limit in number of files or size of the code examples. Use common sense when determining how much of it would someone be ready to read for a quick review.

How to present?

It is easy to point them to a repo and say "There it is!", but as we talked about reducing friction before, here we need to take a similar approach and gently push them in the right direction.

There is no real need to comment every line or to go too much into nitty gritty, but some "author notes" would really help in painting the whole picture behind that code snippet you are presenting.

Video was mentioned before and I see no reason why you could not do an actual presentation and let them inspect the code after? Any code is best presented with come context, and you might be risking misrepresenting the code if left without and guidelines.

> *Whenever providing something you are very familiar with, try to remember that someone else is not. Supply them with enough context in order to ensure proper understanding of the code.*

VI

First Days on the job

You did it! You got the job! But now what?

25

Slow and steady

I vividly recall my first days as if they happened just minutes ago. It's an unforgettable experience, and even if it doesn't go perfectly, there's a strange sense of satisfaction.

You're nervous, meeting new people left and right, everything feels fantastic and flawless! Birds chirp, and the air smells sweeter than ever before.
   Even when I started a new job in my 30s, it felt like the first day of school to me.

This is the payoff for all the hard work and late nights spent studying tutorials that seemed incomprehensible at first, only to try them again in the morning. Embrace this moment, you've earned it!

What I'm about to share may seem counter intuitive or down-right bizarre, but I've witnessed these occurrences regularly among people in my circle, and it's important to address them.

> You **MUST** make sure not to work "too" hard. First month on the job you are setting the expectation and raising the bar. Raise it too high, and you can only go down.

Imagine this scenario:

It's 5 days into your new role, and there's an issue with the app that needs immediate attention before Monday. Do you decline, risking a reputation of unwillingness to help, or do you accept, potentially setting a precedent of working weekends or taking on too much in your first week?

The answer? There isn't a clear one. However, weighing the pros and cons is crucial.

- Is the whole team doing it? Then you have to chip in.
- Do you have plans? Then don't!
- Can you really help at all? Are you knowledgeable enough?
- . . .

The list of examples could continue endlessly, but my advice is simple: listen to your instincts. If you're not feeling up to it and have prior commitments, be honest about it. If the task is within your capabilities and you're eager to contribute, then go ahead and do it!

The key point here is to stay true to yourself. While showing initiative is important and being willing to tackle less appealing tasks is commendable, there should be boundaries.

Expressing your thoughts honestly and acting fairly will earn you respect from your fellow developers, rather than blindly complying with every request that comes your way.

26

Rules of engagement

Over the years, I've established some rules whenever starting a new job or as general guidelines:

- Never work after 5 PM.
- Do not work on weekends.
- If you're sick, prioritize rest over work (seems obvious, right?).
- When idle, offer help to a colleague.
- Use downtime to acquire new skills.

While these rules may appear straightforward, each serves a specific purpose. Let me expand on them a bit.

Never work after 5 PM

If you consistently find yourself staying past 5 o'clock, it may seem odd. Perhaps you need a little extra time to finish up a PR or respond to some emails. Maybe no one has left the office yet, and you'd rather not be the first one out. None of these reasons justify making a habit of working beyond your paid hours.

If you're only staying late to satisfy your internal desire to complete a task, thinking "I could finish it now but post it tomorrow," you might easily slip into the habit of working more than 8 hours. This can give the illusion of increased productivity at the expense of your time, so when you aim to stick to a regular 8-hour workday, it may seem like you've accomplished less.

That's why it's important to expand upon the simple rule of leaving by 5 (or earlier). Continuing to work late can unintentionally signal expectations that are hard to reset moving forward.

Avoid working on weekends.

This might seem obvious, but it's surprising how often new hires fall into this trap while trying to make a good impression. It may feel like having extra time to make that great first impression is an opportunity for advancement, right? Well, it can be, but we must remember not to set unrealistic standards for our future selves—ones who can't maintain a 100% work rate all the time. No company expects this of you and nor should they. Therefore, give your all during work hours, not after.

If you're sick = rest > work

I've been guilty of this several times until I realized that even though I can push through the day and the cold isn't that bad, not only am I setting a bad example but I'm also neglecting self-care. If your body needs rest, allow it to rest – you'll be stronger for it. Continuing to work, even from home, could set a poor example for junior employees or make someone feel guilty for involving you in a meeting while you're unwell.

There's hardly any good reason to work when you're sick.

When idle, offer help to a colleague

Nothing bonds a team quite like collaborating on a problem or dividing the workload for a major task. This approach enables you to learn from others while also sharing your own knowledge – a win-win situation!

An added benefit is that your colleagues may be inspired by your actions and step up to assist you when needed. Cultivating this attitude within the team can foster a positive team culture, and if not already in place, it is likely to catch on swiftly.

Use downtime to acquire new skills

If the previous step didn't prompt anyone to accept help, you can and should focus on learning new things. Once you have a day job, it becomes increasingly challenging to learn new things. It's easy to overlook new technologies or be aware of them but have no time to explore them. This limitation can hinder progress. Remember, setting aside just 30 minutes a day after completing all tasks can make a significant difference in the long run.

> The rules shared above have been effective for me, but it's essential for you to introspect and identify what YOU value most and which priorities you want

to establish. If you truly love what you do and wish to pursue it in your spare time, go for it! Nothing should hinder you from finding joy in your work — you deserve to enjoy it. In simpler terms, be true to yourself.

VII

Future Learning

What to look forward to, for better or worse.

27

KNOW-IT-ALL

Securing your first job is a truly rewarding experience. Initially, it brings feelings of humility and gratitude. However, it also brings a sense of fear of making mistakes and the worry that others will discover your shortcomings sooner or later.

Feeling this way is quite common and completely normal, as most of us harbor uncertainties even when projecting confidence outwardly. Trust me, I appeared confident while secretly spending two entire workdays contemplating whether "git reset —HARD" was an acceptable command to use.

(Spoiler alert: It is.)

After settling in, the inevitable "know-it-all" phase tends to emerge. It's a common human experience. You've just started a new job, submitted a few successful PRs, received positive feedback from colleagues - everything seems to be going well. It's natural to feel proud of yourself!

You deserve to feel good, but this feeling is often fueled by human nature's tendency to warmly embrace newcomers, whether or not it's justified. When I label this as a "culprit," I don't intend it negatively. It's actually a positive aspect, as we should welcome new colleagues with open arms. If this welcoming environment leads to unwarranted confidence, it likely means the individual lacked confidence initially, making it a fair trade-off.

For whatever reason, whether it's hearing about friends still job hunting or seeing people online seeking advice, you feel compelled to share your experience and how you reached success. In that moment, you feel like you're on top of the world, with smooth sailing ahead.

Looking back, it always seems easier to say, "wow, that wasn't so hard," once you've gone through it. Take me, for instance – writing a book about an egg timer app that landed me every job! It took me some time before actually diving into this project. Although I had wanted to share my experience for a while, I held back, thinking I might be oversimplifying the process.

However, after being involved in numerous interviewing processes, I came to realize one thing:

> *People, especially developers, are masters of misrepresenting their work and downplaying their hand. Only a handful was good at this, and coincidentally 100% of them were heavy seniors (10+ years of xp).*
>
> It was at that realization that this book was born, to

give it my best effort in trying to help Junior devs, as all odds were stacked against them.

If that ends up making me sound like a know-it-all so be it.

Takeaway

This stage is temporary, and its effects may vary. Remember the journey you've been on and the hill you've just crossed. While it may seem like a downhill slope for you (in a positive way), someone else might be nearing their peak without realizing it. They could be at the start of their struggles, not knowing what lies ahead.

Therefore, be understanding and supportive of others' struggles. You might just call it "being a good citizen".

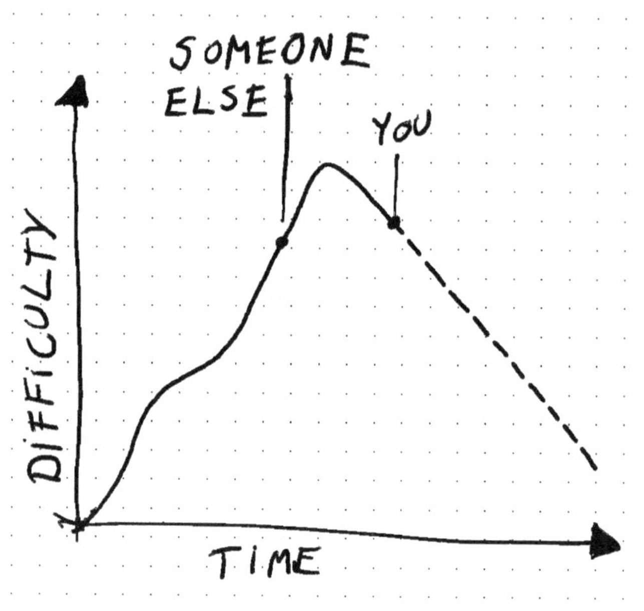
SOMEONE
ELSE
YOU
DIFFICULTY
TIME

28

John Snow

For those who have not seen the "Game Of Thrones" show, there is a very popular quote "...you know nothing John Show", which inspired the naming of this stage.

If we were to draw a learning graph throughout a developers career, it would probably keep going up and down forever. After the initial "know-it-all" phase you will reach the first tip of the graph where you actually realize how much you don't know. You are bound to learn **SOME** things in a wrong way, but **my oh my** now hard it hits when you realize you have almost barely scratched the surface.

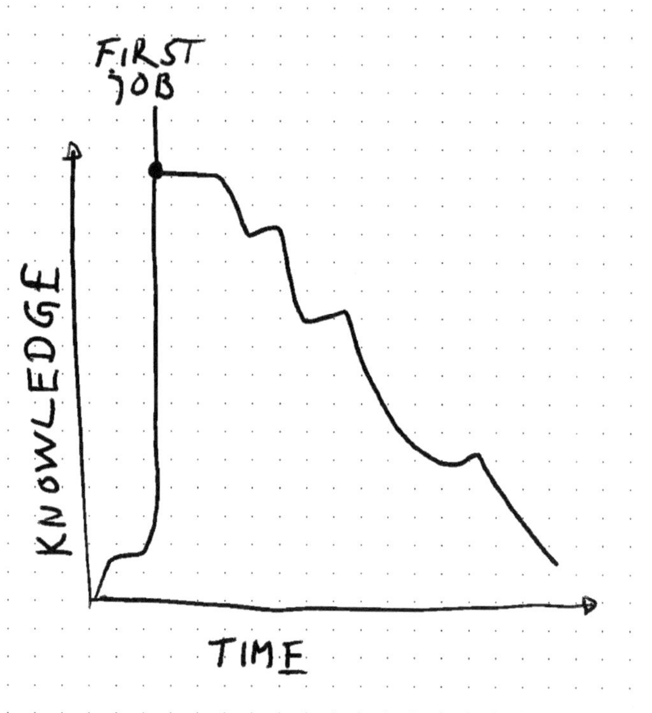

> *It is as if you keep opening doors and behind them you expect a room of a certain size, but it's actually a stadium.*

As time goes on, your assumptions about the room size will become more precise. In my personal opinion, as time progresses, you don't necessarily improve at guessing the room size; instead, you come to accept the fact that **you don't know** what lies ahead.

To some extent, this will happen to everyone. It's almost certain.

The real question is how you handle it. The way you handle it initially is crucial because it can catch you off guard. Reading this will definitely be helpful as it allows you to anticipate and understand what's coming. That's essentially the essence of this book—to prepare you for what lies ahead.

Takeaway

When this does happen, just take a few hours to think about your next steps. Do not panic and start collecting numerous books and courses to quickly fill up the gap before someone notices. Few hours won't hurt, and you need time to reset yourself and re-position for learning that lies ahead.

I use the term "re-position" because the situation you find yourself in reminds me of a challenging section in a game from your childhood. Remember how you used to crack your knuckles, sit up straight, and increase your focus to 105%? Well, this is that stage, that boss level, and that checkpoint.

Take a moment to catch your breath and keep pushing forward. You've got this!

29

Equilibrium

It is difficult to determine how long it would take to reach this stage. However, my best guess is that you would need to go through the previous two stages a few times each to truly feel compelled to move forward.

Nevertheless, it is important to acknowledge that these stages will come and go. What truly matters is to accept them for what they are worth, learn from them, and then move on.

Let me clarify: the previous two stages are not entirely in the past. In fact, one could argue that you can never fully escape them. However, reaching this final stage means that you are capable of adopting a different mindset towards these stages in the future, and perhaps even fast-forwarding through them.

Does it truly matter which stage you find yourself in? Whether you are at a specific point or not, the results will remain the same. The only benefit of knowing about these stages is being aware of their existence and understanding that they are normal. It's similar to recognizing that having a temperature indicates illness and the need for rest. Being able to identify a particular state can certainly offer some peace of mind, if nothing else.

Far be it from me suggesting there are no more than these 3 stages:

- Know-it-all
- John Snow
- Equilibrium

Perhaps you would label them differently, or maybe you would combine them. There might even be stages that I have yet to encounter myself. Each of us experiences personal development in a unique way, and that's why it's important to share our experiences with others. It's the best way to enhance our understanding and truly level up. It's almost like using a cheat code; we not only learn from our own mistakes but also from those of others.

Takeaway

By familiarizing yourself with these stages and having a preliminary understanding of what to expect, I hope that progressing through them will be faster. Soon enough, you'll gain a bird's-eye view of your progress, which can help you avoid occasional tunnel vision.

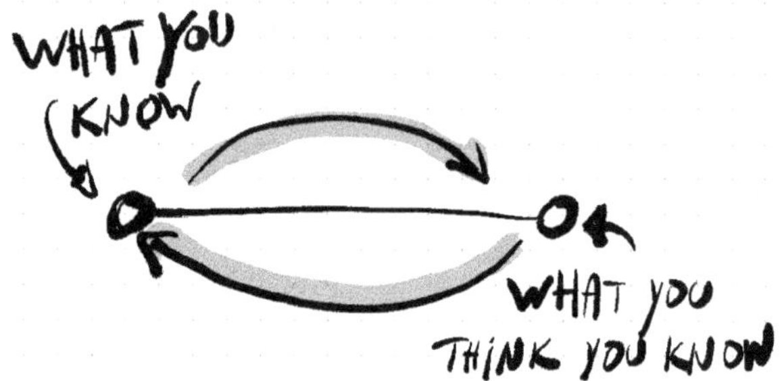
WHAT YOU KNOW
WHAT YOU THINK YOU KNOW

VIII

GLHF

Some last words of advise and to simply wrap up the book.

30

Time to make your mark

I guess this is it! I sincerely hope any of these suggestions will help you on your job hunt. They helped not just me, but a good number of personal friends who asked advice. Even my wife utilized some of these approaches when interviewing and snagged a good job in no-time.

It goes without saying that this is not the ONLY reason that will get you a job and that it works without a fault. However I am very confident that using just some of these approaches will greatly increase your chances of getting that second call.

Going forward and after reading this book, it is up to you to go the extra mile and adapt the approach so it works best for you. Everything in this book is 1:1 how I did interviewing and how I will be doing them in the future. But you are you, and you are more then free to adapt the flow to how it works best for you. Even if this book just inspires you to approach the interviews from a different angle, I consider that a win!

Good luck, you got this!

GOOD LUCK!
-YOU GOT THIS-

The Checklist (a different one)

I thought to include a quick checklist to revise what the whole book is about and to help you consolidate everything once you are ready to start interviewing.

```
[ ] - Make an app
[ ] - Record a short video demo of the app
[ ] - Refactor your CV
[ ] - Investigate the company you are applying to.
Prepare questions.
[ ] - Ensure you are happy with your coverage of the
"Dev Checklist"
[ ] - Let me know on X how your job interview went!
(@emin_ui)
[ ] - Enjoy your new job and help the next person
```

One more thing . . .

I was few seconds away from pushing thing book into stores, where it occurred to me. What best way to learn if not be seeing it live? I have an outdated CV that might require an update and a fresher look, so it would be ideal if I would share how I did that and which tools I used!

So, bellow you will find an unlisted YouTube video on the whole process.

```
https://youtu.be/HSd05in8-SU
```

This book will be printed as well, so sorry for not finding a good way to share that on paper.

Tools used:

- VEED.io
- iPhone native screen record capability
- ffmpeg terminal command

This is the code I used to fuse the videos together, I just hope it will stand the test of time. If it is outdated, or you have issues with it, you know where to find me! (@emin_ui)

```
ffmpeg -i leftVideo.mp4 -i rightVideo.mp4
-filter_complex
"[1:v]pad=iw:1792:(ow-iw)/2:(oh-ih)/2:black[pad];[0:v]
[pad]hstack=inputs=2[v]" -map "[v]" -map 1:a -c:a
copy output.mp4
```

:Waving emoji:

I think this is it. To be honest makes me kind of sad to be done with the book, but I will be expanding it and improving it as I learn new things and as new technologies come around.

It has been fun! I do hope this book helps you get a job or at least motivates you to have a think about how you present yourself in an interview.

As I mentioned so many times already, do get in touch via X (@emin_ui), and let's have a chat! Now, get out there, send those CV's and get hired!

Good Luck! You Got This!

GO!

* 9 7 8 8 2 3 0 3 6 6 6 0 8 *